THE ROLE OF FEMALE UNION SPIES IN THE CIVIL WAR

Warrior Women in American History

THE ROLE OF FEMALE UNION SPIES IN THE CIVIL WAR

Cavendish
Square

New York

Hallie Murray

Published in 2020 by Cavendish Square Publishing, LLC

243 5th Avenue, Suite 136, New York, NY 10016

Copyright © 2020 by Cavendish Square Publishing, LLC

First Edition

Website: cavendishsq.com

This publication represents the opinions and views of the author based on his or her personal experience, knowledge, and research. The information in this book serves as a general guide only. The author and publisher have used their best efforts in preparing this book and disclaim liability rising directly or indirectly from the use and application of this book.

All websites were available and accurate when this book was sent to press.

Cataloging-in-Publication Data
Names: Murray, Hallie.
Title: The role of female Union spies in the Civil War / Hallie Murray.
Description: New York : Cavendish Square Publishing, 2020. | Series: Warrior
    women in American history | Includes glossary and index.
Identifiers: ISBN 9781502655523 (pbk.) | ISBN 9781502655530 (library bound) |
    ISBN 9781502655547 (ebook)
Subjects: LCSH: Women spies–United States–Biography–Juvenile literature. | Spies-
    -United States–Biography–Juvenile literature. | United States–History–Civil War,
    1861-1865–Secret service–Biography–Juvenile literature. | United States–History-
    -Civil War, 1861-1865–Participation, Female–Juvenile literature. | United States–
    History–Civil War, 1861-1865–Biography–Juvenile literature.
Classification: LCC E608.M87 2020 | DDC 973.7'850922 B–dc23

Printed in China

Portions of this book originally appeared in *Women Civil War Spies of the Union* by Lois Sakany.

Contents

Introduction

Though the American Civil War officially began in April 1861, the division between the sides that would become the Union and the Confederacy had been growing for some time, going back to even before the American Revolution. The issue centered on slavery: many people, particularly those who lived in Northern states, believed slavery was wrong and should be outlawed. Northern states depended much more on manufacturing, whereas the South depended much more on agriculture, which required enormous amounts of labor. Those from Southern states, whose economies therefore depended on slavery to produce that labor, believed their states would descend into financial ruin if the practice were made illegal.

Southern politicians were particularly worried about presidential candidate Abraham Lincoln. They believed he was against slavery and were so afraid of what he might do that they threatened to secede if he became president. When Lincoln was elected in 1860, they made good on that threat. One by one, Southern states began to secede from the Union, beginning with South Carolina in December 1860. These states together formed the Confederate States of America.

The federal government, however, didn't accept the newly formed Confederacy. Lincoln and other politicians asserted that secession was illegal, and no other nations recognized the Confederacy as a sovereign state. If the

Abraham Lincoln, who is shown here in 1860, was elected president a time when tensions were running high in the United States.

Confederacy wanted to fully sever itself from the Union and become its own country, it would have to do so by force. The only way forward, it seemed, was war. On April 12, 1861, Confederate troops attacked the federal fort of Fort Sumter in South Carolina, and the four-year conflict that would become the bloodiest war in America's history officially began.

Prior to and during the Civil War, women were not allowed to hold office, fight in the military, or even vote. In fact, the only role women were really supposed to play in a conflict like the Civil War was supporting their husbands, fathers, and sons in the war effort. But women have never been content to sit at home while battles rage—women have participated in every war in history, whether in an official or unofficial capacity. In the Civil War, some women on both the Union and Confederate sides participated by dressing as men and going to fight. Others acted as nurses or doctors, aiding the sick and wounded, or helped gather supplies and organize relief efforts. But many other women worked behind the scenes, helping the cause more quietly and sneakily, acting as spies.

Since women during the Civil War were never officially hired by the military to carry out their acts of espionage, there is little record of their service. Today, only a handful of their stories remain—those that survived through written records made either during the war or shortly thereafter—and much of the secret work that was carried out by women has remained hidden. Women who acted as spies or scouts during the Civil War had little to gain by shedding light on their stories. As the biographies in this book demonstrate, even women whose service was

Frances L. Clalin was one of the few women known to have disguised herself as a man to fight for the Union during the Civil War.

recognized by military and political leaders struggled to receive any sort of compensation.

In addition, female spies who made their activities known were often judged as eccentric—if not freakish—for taking on work that was deemed inappropriate for women. And while the Union may have won the war, it did not win the hearts of most Confederates. As a result, it was downright dangerous for a Southerner who spied for the Union to reveal her activities after the war ended.

Certainly, many of the women involved in passing on information never viewed themselves as spies. They simply saw an opportunity to help the cause. In the aftermath of the war, those who were spies or operatives were not necessarily proud of their acts of deception but rather viewed them as an unpleasant but necessary part of war. In looking at the many Civil War spy stories, it is difficult to categorize the women who chose to serve their country as secret agents. Their socioeconomic classes varied tremendously, ranging from slaves who owned nothing to women who were exceedingly wealthy. From a geographic perspective, Union spies claimed birthplaces that ranged from the Deep South to Canada. Many women who spied did so because they were opposed to slavery, though some simply believed in the preservation of the Union.

If nothing else, they were women of conviction. Like many women throughout history, they were not afraid to take a stand on issues in which they strongly believed. For all of them, there were great risks involved in their missions. Despite the substantial challenges and danger, these women were not cowed into submission and instead made the heroic choice not only to have an opinion but also to act on it.

The Union's Angel of Revenge

Though it was the last state to secede, Tennessee saw more than its fair share of battles during the Civil War, located as it was on the border of the Union and the Confederacy. Perhaps for the same reason, politics in Tennessee were deeply divided. Many Tennessee residents supported secession, but a sizable portion remained loyal to the Union. One of those Tennessee Unionists was Sarah E. Thompson, who, along with her husband Sylvanius, organized recruitment efforts for the Union army. After Sylvanius was killed by Confederate general John Hunt Morgan, Thompson continued to support the Union by acting as a courier, conducting intelligence operations, and later serving as a nurse in the federal army. And when General Morgan returned to her town, Thompson avenged her husband by bringing him down.

Secret Union Supporters in Tennessee

Sarah Lane was born in Green County, Tennessee, on February 11, 1838, twenty-three years before the start of the Civil War. When she was sixteen, she married Sylvanius H. Thompson, and they had two daughters. When the war began, Tennessee remained split between loyalty to the Union and to the Confederacy. Though the state would eventually secede in 1861, many residents supported the

The Third Indiana Cavalry poses together in Petersburg, Virginia. Cavalry soldiers fought on horseback, usually armed with pistols or swords. The men here hold sabers (swords) by their sides.

Union cause, particularly in East Tennessee, where the Thompsons lived. As a family, the Thompsons remained loyal to the Union cause.

Not long after the war began, Thompson's husband became a private for the Union in the Tennessee Calvary. By then, Tennessee had already seceded from the Union, and Sylvanius had to travel several days to Barberville, Kentucky, in order to sign on with the Union army. He was enrolled on July 12, 1862, and was subsequently sent back to Tennessee to serve as an army recruiter. By all accounts, Sarah and Sylvanius's marriage was happy, and the two spent as much time together as possible. After Sylvanius joined the military, whenever she could, Thompson assisted him in his recruitment efforts. Together they enlisted about five hundred men.

The number may not seem so large until one considers that the Thompsons were recruiting members for the

Union army in a state that had declared its loyalties to the Confederacy. They had to recruit in secret through a network of trustworthy friends and acquaintances. When a sufficient number of men had signed up to serve, Sylvanius would provide them with a confidential meeting place and time. They would then travel in secret across the state line to Kentucky, where the men were sworn into the Union army.

Thompson assisted Sylvanius on other assignments, too, and she later wrote about the bond of trust that existed between them:

> [Sylvanius] came to help the union men escape from the wrath of the enemy and he had to stay in a secret place and keep himself hid. As a matter of course, someone had to help him and as he had more confidence in me than anyone else, he asked me to aid him.[1]

Tragedy Strikes

While on a dispatch to deliver a message to General Ambrose Burnside, who was stationed at the time in Knoxville, Tennessee, Sylvanius was captured. He was transported to Belle Island Prison in Richmond, Virginia, where he managed to escape after a few months. He soon returned to Tennessee, where he rejoined his regiment.

In January 1864, while on another delivery mission for the general, Sylvanius was captured again, this time by Confederate soldiers under General John Hunt Morgan. But Sylvanius would not be sent back to prison for a second offense. Instead, he was executed.

Sarah Thompson, meanwhile, had continued to work for the Union, recruiting soldiers and delivering dispatches.

Though Thompson was heartbroken when she heard the news of her husband's death, his passing also inspired her. In a letter she wrote long after the end of the war, she recalled Sylvanius's death: "While returning from a mission, he was captured by Morgan's guerrillas and shot. Having thus been widowed, I devoted all my strength and energy to aid the cause."[2] Thompson swore she would make the Confederacy pay for her husband's death.

She didn't have to wait long. Less than a year after her husband was executed, Thompson heard through the grapevine that General Morgan had recently arrived in Greenville. Morgan was well known for his use of guerrilla tactics to make daring raids on Union-held cities in both the North and South, and he had a bad reputation with many Union loyalists. Thompson wasn't the only one who wanted him dead.

Thompson Enacts Her Revenge

The Union could not have been more delighted when Morgan was captured during the summer of 1863. Unfortunately, he soon escaped with six of his men in November 1863. It's not clear why Morgan returned to Greenville in 1864. Some accounts say that he was there with 1,600 of his men, preparing for another raid. Whatever Morgan's reasons were, while he was in Greenville, he stayed with the Williamses, family friends who lived in a large mansion near the center of town. His arrival in Greenville was newsworthy, and it wasn't long before Thompson knew exactly where he was staying.

Since she wasn't sure just how long Morgan would remain in Greenville, Thompson immediately began working on a plan to reveal his whereabouts to a large

The facial hairstyle called "sideburns" is named after General Ambrose Burnside, a leader of the Union army during the Civil War.

force of federal cavalry stationed just outside of town. However, in order to deliver the messages, she would first have to figure out a way to get past the Confederate soldiers guarding all roads out of town.

Luckily, Thompson was acquainted with a Confederate captain whose family lived in Greenville. Thompson asked him if he could obtain permission from one of the sentries to let her pass so she could milk one of the cows grazing nearby. Recalling the event in a diary, Thompson wrote, "I asked him to pass me out after my cow, as there was several cows on the hill, and he told the guard to pass me out and to pass me in when I returned and I would give him some milk."[3]

Ambrose Burnside

A well-known Union general, Ambrose Burnside was born in Indiana in May 1824. He began is military career at the United States Military Academy and went on to serve in various positions throughout the Western frontier until he was assigned to Rhode Island in 1852. Soon after the Civil War began, Burnside was appointed major general of volunteers for the Union army in recognition of his success in a number of battles in Virginia. Unfortunately, he ran into a string of bad luck and made some poor decisions, which eventually resulted in his being removed from command. After the war, Burnside served as governor of Rhode Island from 1866 to 1869 and as senator from Rhode Island from 1875 to 1881. Outside of his military and government service, Burnside is also remembered for being the namesake of sideburns, which were initially called "burnsides" in recognition of his unique facial hair.

JOHN MORGAN.

General John Hunt Morgan was a military leader with the Confederacy. Though initially not a supporter of secession, Morgan became a symbol of the push to bring Kentucky into the Confederacy.

Once she passed the guard, Thompson raced to a friend's house, where she was able to borrow a horse. It was near midnight when she finally reached the camp. Awoken from sleep, Major General Alvan Gillem, the commander in charge, did not at first believe her report on Morgan's whereabouts. However, two officers on his staff confirmed that Thompson had been a reliable source of information in the past.

Morgan's Death

One hundred Union cavalrymen were immediately selected to ride into Greenville and recapture Morgan. Although Thompson must have been exhausted from the long and dangerous trip, she did not want to leave anything to chance by staying behind. Concerned that Morgan might leave the mansion before they returned, Thompson had made arrangements so that he could not escape undetected. Besides, Thompson was not about to miss witnessing the demise of the man who was at least partially responsible for her husband's death.

Larry G. Eggleston writes: "General Morgan was still asleep when the Union troops swept in to Greenville just prior to dawn. When the alarm was sounded by one of the sentries, Morgan was shaken awake by his guards. Quickly donning a pair of pants over his nightclothes, he hurried downstairs and asked Mrs. Williams where the Yankees were. 'Everywhere,' she replied."[4]

As Thompson suspected, Morgan was tipped off that the cavalry was coming and escaped before their arrival. But Thompson was well prepared for this. She had paid another woman to watch Morgan, and when Thompson found Morgan had disappeared, the other woman

19

This woodcut offers an artist's interpretation of a confrontation between Confederate and Union cavalry, with significant bloodshed as soldiers on horseback charge at one another with swords.

informed her that Morgan was hidden in a nearby vineyard. Thompson told the nearest Union soldier she could find, and within minutes, Morgan was discovered. He refused to surrender and was shot and killed on the spot.

In the days following Morgan's death, chaos ensued, and Thompson was captured and held prisoner in her own home. Her captors threatened to hang her. They told her that her hanged body would be displayed for at least three days. But Thompson was rescued by members of the Union army, and because there was a reward for her capture, she left Greenville. First, she relocated to Knoxville, Tennessee, then to Cleveland, Ohio, where she served as a nurse until the war ended.

Making Ends Meet

In 1879, Thompson wrote a letter to US secretary of the treasury John Sherman, seemingly to ask for financial assistance. In making a case for how useful she'd been to the Union during the war, Thompson summarized her wartime accomplishments:

> I obtained [information] concerning the actual and intended movements, strength and disposition of the rebel forces. [I] led union men desiring to enlist into the federal lines. [I] was the frequent bearer of secret dispatches between commanding officers. [I] gave Federal officers the information of Morgan's presence in Greenville, which lead to his defeat and death. [I] was given three hours notice to abandon my home and proclaimed a Union spy by [Confederate president] Jefferson Davis, who authorized a reward for my arrest. After which, I served as a nurse in Knoxville and Cleveland, where I remained as a nurse until the close of the war.[5]

Unfortunately, no money was granted to her at that time. After the war, she supported herself by giving lectures in Northern cities about her wartime activities, but there was little money to be made speaking about such accomplishments.

A year after the war ended, Thompson married Orville J. Bacon. They had two children, but the marriage was short and ended with Orville's early death from an illness. On her own once again and now with four children to support, Thompson struggled to make ends meet. In an effort to receive compensation for her services during the war, Thompson repeatedly wrote letters to influential members of the government and the military, pleading her case. Her efforts paid off in the form of a clerical job with the Treasury Department, for which she was paid $600 per year.

In the 1880s, Thompson married James Cotton, who, like her previous two husbands, died soon after they were wed. Her efforts to receive compensation for her service during the war finally paid off in 1899, when, by special action of Congress, Thompson was granted a pension of $12 per month.

When she turned sixty-five, she retired from her government position. She was living with her son Orville Bacon Jr. at the time and was going to visit him at his job one afternoon when she was hit by a trolley. Thompson died from her injuries on April 21, 1909. She was buried in Arlington National Cemetery in Washington, DC, with full military honors.

The Abolitionist Southern Belle

Union spy Elizabeth Van Lew was born into a wealthy family in Richmond, Virginia. She used her connections and privilege to gather information from people of all classes during the Civil War. Though she considered herself a Southern woman through and through, Van Lew was vehemently against slavery, and when her father died, she freed the family's slaves and used the money she'd inherited to purchase and free as many of their relatives as she could.

During the Civil War, Van Lew created and maintained a wide-ranging spy ring, whose members included servants, slaves, clerks in the Confederate government, and even Richmond politicians. Van Lew herself also collected information from prisoners at Libby Prison and from other wealthy socialites at parties. Unfortunately, after the war, many citizens of Richmond were angry with Van Lew for supporting the Union, and she had little money at the end of her life, having used all of her inheritance to further her abolitionist activities and finance intelligence operations during the war.

A Radical and Headstrong Heiress

Van Lew was born on October 12, 1818, in Richmond, Virginia, to an affluent, slave-owning family. She was the

Though Elizabeth Van Lew's family owned slaves, Van Lew herself was educated at a Quaker school in Philadelphia and became an abolitionist like her maternal grandfather, Hilary Baker.

eldest of John and Elizabeth Van Lew's three children. Her father, John Van Lew, grew up in Long Island, but he left Long Island after his business failed and moved south to Richmond, where he and a partner began a hardware business. Because the store was unique to the South, it was very successful. Soon, the Van Lews became wealthy and were well regarded in Richmond society.

Van Lew's mother, the former Elizabeth Louis Baker, was born in Philadelphia, where the young Van Lew was sent for her formal education. It is believed that there Van Lew first formed her opinions about slavery, to which she was opposed from an early age. "Slave power degrades labor," she wrote in her journal. "Slave power is arrogant, is jealous and intrusive, is cruel, is despotic, not only over the slave, but over the community, the state."[1]

However, the beginnings of her heartfelt views were probably in place long before she entered any classroom. In her journal, Van Lew describes herself as "tolerant and uncompromising, but liberal, quick in feeling, and ready to resent what seemed to me wrong—quick and passionate but not bad tempered or vicious. This has made my life sad and earnest."[2] As such, Van Lew was never shy about informing those who knew her about her opinions. She frequently argued about slavery with her father, insisting that he free the nine slaves owned by the family.

Van Lew's pleas were ignored, but in the end, she was able to get her way. When Van Lew's father died when she was in her mid-twenties, she promptly liberated the family's slaves. Some of them left, while others stayed on as paid workers. Using her inheritance money, she also set about freeing the relatives of those who were now employed by her.

War Comes to Richmond

Though a proud Virginian, Van Lew was dismayed when talk of secession rumbled through Richmond. It was around this same time that Van Lew began her pro-North activities by corresponding with federal officials and letting them know about happenings in Richmond.

When Virginia seceded in the spring of 1861, Van Lew and her mother were called upon to aid the Confederate cause. They flatly refused but were eventually forced to comply under the duress of personal threats. The henchmen who pushed her into service would have done better to ban Van Lew forever from partaking in any wartime activities instead of inserting her in the middle of them. Rather than sitting quietly at home, Van Lew now had a direct line on confidential information about the Confederacy's war plans, which she promptly turned over to the federal government.

In the early days of the war, Van Lew and her mother fulfilled their obligations by bringing religious books to prison camps. After the first land battle of the war, the Battle of Big Bethel, on June 10, 1861, federal prisoners began to arrive in Richmond. Van Lew was struck by the poor treatment they were receiving and volunteered to supply them with food, clothing, and medicine. While bringing in supplies, she also managed to gather intelligence from the prison guards as well as the prisoners, who had been brought through Confederate lines on the way to Richmond.

The people of Richmond grew increasingly angry with her visits to enemy prison camps, but Van Lew was undeterred. The act of freeing the family's slaves, along with her sympathy for the Union military, earned her the nickname of Crazy Bet among the townspeople.

The original caption for this image of Libby Prison, dated August 23, 1863, claims that this is "the only picture in existence" of the structure. Libby Prison gained a reputation for keeping Union officers in extremely poor conditions.

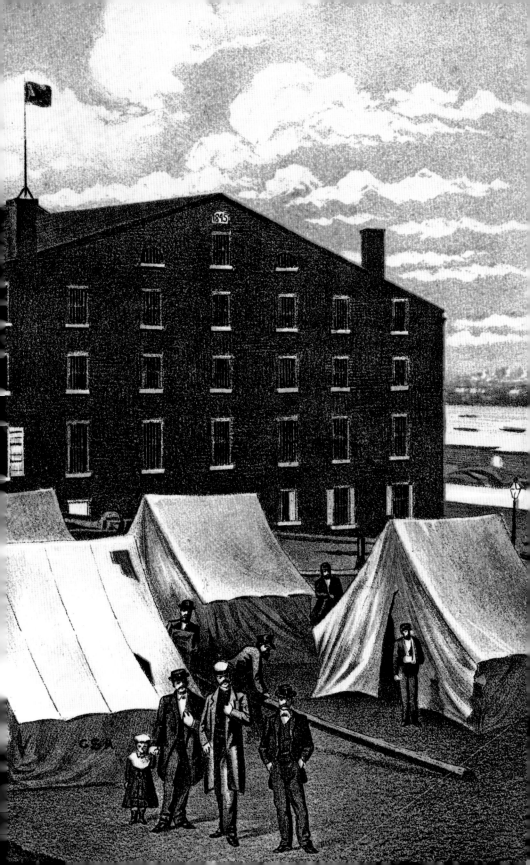

Van Lew viewed the moniker as an advantage and played up the role of the "crazy" old lady whenever she was in public. While the residents of Richmond may have disliked her activities, a disheveled woman who mumbled loudly while going about her errands was less likely to be suspected of committing espionage.

Secrets and Spying

While the city's residents entertained themselves by gossiping about Crazy Bet, she kept herself busy by widening the reach of her covert operations and reporting to her Union contacts under the code name Babcock. In addition to the work she carried out with her mother at the prisons, Van Lew also gathered information through a wide network that included her own employees as well as slaves who were still in bondage. The editor of her diary wrote of these operations: "Information was delivered by servants carrying baskets of eggs. One egg in each basket was hollow and contained her notes, which she had torn into small pieces. In addition, notes were carried in the soles of the servants' shoes."[3]

Van Lew also used her society connections to gather information on the Confederates. As a member of Richmond's upper class, she often hosted parties in her own home for Richmond's high-ranking Confederate officials and other elite families. The commander of a Richmond prison, Lieutenant David H. Todd, whose half sister was the wife of Abraham Lincoln, was one of Van Lew's closest friends. After Lieutenant Todd was reassigned, she befriended his replacement commander, who, along with his family, became boarders living in the Van Lew mansion.

Friends in High Places

Though those who acted covertly often had a reputation for reporting information that was exaggerated, Van Lew was known for the accuracy of the information she gathered. Her solid reputation meant that she communicated with "some of the Federal government's highest-ranking officers, including George H. Sharp, chief of the U.S. Bureau of Military Information, Benjamin Butler, commander of the Army of the James, George G. Mead, commander of the Army of the Potomac, and Ulysses S. Grant, commander of the Union forces."[4] These men were at the very top of the intelligence chain, and the fact that Van Lew reported directly to them meant that she herself was placed quite high up. This is further evidenced by her significant network of spies and informants—Van Lew was able to collect information from every sort of person living in Richmond, piecing together knowledge from all places in order to create an accurate picture of the situation.

Despite Van Lew's awareness that she was being watched closely by operatives for the Confederates, she remained fearless, carrying on a number of risky operations, including running a spy ring, within the confines of her home. The mansion was a well-known safe house in which Van Lew frequently hid runaway slaves and prisoners en route to the North. Among the many sections of her house was a large secret room that once hid more than one hundred men.

The Union Victory at Richmond

In April 1865, after repeated attempts, the federal army overtook Richmond. In an act that could be considered

Ulysses S. Grant, pictured here circa 1865, served as commanding general of the Union army and was president of the United States from 1869 to 1877.

either extremely brave or extremely foolish, Van Lew had an American flag smuggled through the lines, and when Richmond surrendered, she and her servants climbed up to the roof of the house and raised it. It was the first American flag to be displayed in Richmond since the start of the war.

The sight of the flag enraged Van Lew's neighbors, and many of them gathered on her lawn and shouted threats at her. She defiantly opened her door and yelled, "General Grant will be here in one hour. I know all of you, and if you harm me or my property your homes will be burned to the ground by noon."[5]

When General Grant arrived, he offered his thanks to Van Lew during a visit to her home, where he stationed several soldiers to guard her and the mansion. Van Lew was ecstatic. In her journal, she wrote, "What a moment! The chains, the shackles fell from thousands of captives. Civilization advanced a century. Justice, truth, humanity were vindicated. Labor was now without manacles, honored and respected. Oh, army of my country, how glorious was your welcome!"[6]

Following the conflict, General George H. Sharp proposed that Van Lew be appropriated $15,000 for her efforts during the war. In a letter, he wrote about Van Lew's "system of correspondence in cipher by which specific information asked for by General [Grant] was obtained."[7]

Postwar Isolation

The Van Lew family received less compensation for their efforts. In 1869, fifteen days after Grant was inaugurated as president, he appointed Van Lew postmaster of Richmond. She received an annual salary of $1,200, which she sorely needed, as she had often used her own funds to finance her spying activities. As a result, she had been nearly penniless by the end of the war.

The citizens of Richmond resented Van Lew's appointment, and as more information on her wartime activities surfaced, her unpopularity increased. She spent the final years of her life ostracized by those around her. In a letter to John H. Forbes, a former Union solder who helped her financially in her later years, she wrote, "I live here in the most perfect isolation with my niece. We have no friendly visits, except that once or twice a year two families call. You know the women have never forgiven me."[8] When her mother died in 1875, she wrote another acquaintance that she did not have enough friends to serve as pallbearers.

Van Lew died on September 25, 1900, at the age of eighty-two. At the time of her death, she was destitute. Her funeral was attended by a handful of family members, servants, and relatives of the Union soldiers she had helped during the war. She was buried in Shockoe Hill Cemetery in Richmond. Years later, relatives of Colonel Paul Revere (a descendant of the famous Revolutionary War patriot), whom she had helped escape from prison, purchased a headstone, which reads, "She risked everything that is dear to man—friends, fortune, comfort, health and life itself. All for one absorbing desire of her heart—that slavery might be abolished and the Union preserved."[9]

It is likely that she would have appreciated the kind words that grace her headstone. The journal entries Van Lew wrote following the war indicate that she felt her wartime efforts were not appreciated. One of her final journal entries reflects these mixed feelings:

Van Lew's grave is located in Shockoe Hill Cemetery in Richmond, Virginia. Her former home was demolished in 1911, and an elementary school was built on the grounds.

If I am entitled to the name of "Spy" because I was in the secret service, I accept it willingly; but it will hereafter have to my mind a high and honorable signification. For my loyalty to my country I have two beautiful names—here I am called, "Traitor," farther North a "spy"—instead of the honored name of "Faithful."[10]

In the House of the Enemy

Since they lived and worked in such close proximity to their masters, slaves and servants, especially those owned or employed by prominent Confederate leaders, were a crucial source of information for Union intelligence gathering. One of these key informants was Mary Elizabeth Bowser, a former slave in the Van Lew household who was freed when Elizabeth Van Lew's father died. After she was freed, Bowser was sent to Philadelphia to study at the Quaker School for Negroes, and when she returned, Van Lew inducted Bowser into her spy ring.

Bowser is perhaps best known for her work spying on Confederate president Jefferson Davis. Van Lew had convinced a friend to allow Bowser to work Confederate functions at President Davis's mansion, and after a few of these events at the mansion, Davis's wife decided that Bowser would be excellent as a staff servant. Bowser worked for the Davis family from 1863 until the end of the Civil War. According to several accounts, she had a photographic memory and put it to good use reporting on the Confederate president's activities.

The Other Van Lews

Mary Elizabeth Bowser was born sometime around 1839 to parents who were slaves on a plantation owned by John Van Lew, father of Elizabeth Van Lew.

Quaker Resistance

Quakers were known for opposing slavery, and stops along the Underground Railroad were often homes and barns owned by Quakers. One such Quaker was Virginia schoolteacher Rebecca Wright. Writes Elaine Schneider: "One day after class, Rebecca opened her door to Thomas Laws, a black man posing as a peddler. Once within her home and away from prying eyes, the old man pulled a written message from his mouth. The paper read: 'Ms. Wright, I know that you are a loyal lady and still love the old flag. Can you inform me of the position of rebel troops and their probable intentions?' The note was signed by General Phillip Sheridan of the Union army."[1] Wright wasn't a spy, but she recalled overhearing a conversation between two Confederate soldiers in town. Her information was key to Sheridan's decision to attack immediately, which enabled him to win the Third Battle of Winchester.

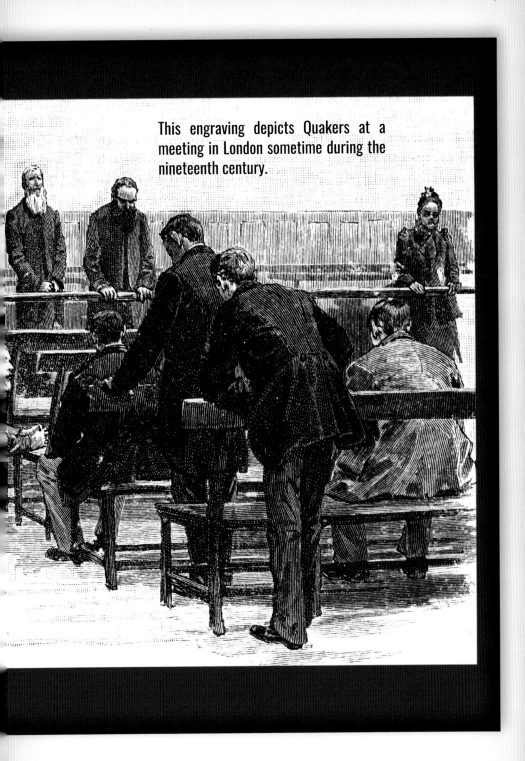

This engraving depicts Quakers at a meeting in London sometime during the nineteenth century.

The exact date of her birth is not known. Lacking the rights of citizens, slaves were viewed as less important than whites, and their slave masters saw little reason to record the official details of their lives.

When John Van Lew died in 1843, his oldest daughter, Elizabeth, who was outspoken in her distaste for the institution of slavery, freed all nine of the family's slaves. Most left the Van Lew plantation, though some, including Mary Elizabeth Bowser's parents, chose to remain as hired farmhands and house servants. Mary Elizabeth, who was a young girl at the time, stayed with her parents. When she turned ten, Van Lew sent her to be educated at the Quaker School for Negroes in Philadelphia.

Not long after she finished her schooling, she married Wilson Bowser, a free black man. The wedding ceremony took place on April 16, 1861, at St. John's Church in Richmond, in front of an audience of white parishioners. This formal marriage ceremony between two blacks in front of a white audience was very unusual in the South.

Bowser's marriage took place just four days after the attack on Fort Sumter and one day before Virginia left the Union. After Virginia seceded, Elizabeth Van Lew began providing the federal government with a steady stream of information about the Confederacy's military plans and actions near Richmond, as was explained in the previous chapter. As the war escalated, Van Lew simply expanded what was already a large network of spies and operatives.

A Spy in the Home

Details about how Bowser became a spy for Van Lew are sketchy. The two remained close after Bowser completed her education, though it is not clear where Bowser was living or working when Van Lew called on her to become a part of her spy network. In any case, given that Bowser was a free woman married to a free man, it is a testament to her commitment to end slavery as well as her trust in Van Lew that she would agree to take on such a dangerous role.

It is not clear who came up with the idea to plant Bowser as a servant spy in the Richmond home of Confederacy president Jefferson Davis. It is known, however, that in 1862 Bowser and Van Lew put the plan into action. Though Van Lew herself wasn't friendly with the Davises, she was well acquainted with several people who were frequent guests at their home. Van Lew knew of one such visitor who was a Union sympathizer, and she managed to persuade her to take Bowser to assist at functions at the Davis mansion. Though Bowser was intelligent and well educated, all agreed that she would arouse less suspicion if she took on the role of a slow-witted and obedient servant.

After a few events at the mansion, the friend encouraged Davis's wife, Varina Davis, to hire Bowser as a servant. Varina Davis agreed, and Bowser assisted the Davis family from 1863 until just before the end of the war. While Bowser cleaned and cooked, she also waited on Jefferson Davis and his military leaders. In doing so, she was able to read war dispatches and overhear conversations about the movements and strategies of Confederate troops. She memorized this information and told it to other spies who coded it and sent it to General Ulysses S. Grant and General Benjamin Butler, "'greatly enhancing the Union's conduct of the war,' according to the account assembled by the U.S. Army Military Intelligence Corps Hall of Fame."[2]

Jefferson Davis served in Congress and as secretary of war under Franklin Pierce. He was the first and only president of the Confederate States of America.

A Hidden History

Very little is known about where Bowser went or what she did after the war. The date and place of her death are unknown, which reflects both her status as a black woman and her work as an undercover agent. In an effort to protect those who were part of her espionage network, Van Lew didn't record the names or activities of her operatives in the journal she kept during the war. Further confounding efforts to find written proof of Bowser's activities, Van Lew asked that the War Department destroy all of the messages she had sent during the war. While Van Lew's decision to keep Bowser's actions secret was no doubt a wise one, the lack of written proof led to some controversy.

Jefferson Davis

Jefferson Davis was born in Kentucky in 1809, though he grew up in Mississippi. He spent six years in the military before leaving the service in 1835 in order to marry his commanding officer's daughter. She passed away soon after they were married, and a devastated Davis receded from the public eye and focused on developing his brother's plantation. In 1845, he married Varina Howell and became a congressman for Mississippi. In 1853, he became the United States secretary of war. Though Davis didn't actually support secession, he did support each state's *right* to secede. After the Civil War began, he was soon appointed major general of the Army of Mississippi. He was then chosen as the president of the Confederacy by military and government leaders, and he served in that position from 1861 to the end of the war in 1865.

Davis's first wife, Sarah Knox Taylor, died in 1835, just months after their marriage. He met his second wife, Varina Howell, pictured with Davis here, in 1844. They married in 1845 and had six children together.

The "White House of the Confederacy," located in Richmond, Virginia, was the executive home of Jefferson and Varina Davis while Jefferson Davis served as president of the Confederacy.

The absence of a written record has led to some doubt as to whether Bowser really acted as a spy within the Davis household, though most historians agree that Bowser contributed to the war effort.

When her former Richmond home was opened as the Confederate Museum in 1896, Varina Davis spoke fondly of her faithful slaves, but she said nothing about the issue of treachery and spies. However, after Van Lew's death in 1900, stories regarding Bowser's activities in the Davis house resurfaced. Perhaps hoping to save face and put these rumors to rest, Varina Davis wrote to museum head Isabel Maury and denied them all. In a note dated April 17, 1905, written from her New York hotel, Davis discussed the subject:

> My daughter has sent me your letter of inquiry to know if I had in my employ

an educated negro woman whose services were "given or hired by Miss Van Lew" as a spy in our house during the war. We never had any such person about us. I had no "educated negro" in my household. My maid was an ignorant girl born and brought up on our plantation who if she is living now, I am sure cannot read, and who would not have done anything to injure her master or me if even she had been educated. That Miss Van Lew may have been imposed upon by some educated negro woman's tales I am quite prepared to believe.

Very truly yours,
Varina Jefferson Davis[3]

When faced with the possibility that she was responsible for such a colossal blunder, it comes as no surprise that Davis hotly denied the stories. What she perhaps knowingly failed to address in her letter is the likelihood that her maid was none other than Bowser putting on a fine performance as "an ignorant girl,"[4] all the while gathering critical information on Confederate operations.

Uncovering the Truth

Despite Davis's denials, some of Bowser's activities were confirmed by Thomas McNiven, who owned a bakery in Richmond and, sometimes in cooperation with Van Lew, operated an espionage network. Though McNiven kept a journal, it was destroyed by the executor of his will after his death in the early 1900s. However, in 1952, his grandson Robert Waitt had the wisdom to record the memories of

McNiven's wartime activities as told to him by McNiven's oldest daughter.

Regarding McNiven's network of operatives, his daughter recalled her father's description of Bowser: "Van Lew's colored girl, Mary, was the best as she was working right in Jefferson Davis's home and [she] had a photographic mind. Everything she saw on the Rebel president's desk she could repeat word for word. She made a point of always coming out to my wagon when I made deliveries at the Davis' home to drop information."[5]

Within Bowser's own family, little mention was made of her wartime activities. The desire to protect her even after her death is illustrated in a comment made by McEva Bowser (the wife of Mary's grandnephew) when asked by a cousin in the 1960s if she had ever heard of Mary Bowser. She replied, "No, never heard of her. Well, they don't ever talk about her 'cause she was a spy."[6]

According to McEva Bowser, she came across what appeared to be Bowser's diary when her husband's mother died:

> I was cleaning her room and I ran across a diary, but I never had a diary and I didn't even realize what it was. And I did keep coming across [references to] Mr. Davis. And the only Davis I could think of was the contractor who had been doing some work at the house. And the first time I came across it, I threw it aside and said I would read it again. Then I started to talk to my husband about it but I felt it would depress him. So the next time I came across it I just pitched it in the trash can.[7]

In spite of the lack of printed material confirming Bowser's service as a spy, the US Army concluded that there was sufficient evidence to induct her into the Military Intelligence Corps Hall of Fame on June 30, 1995, for her duties during the Civil War. The army's tribute to her read, "Ms. Bowser certainly succeeded in a highly dangerous mission to the great benefit of the Union effort. She was one of the highest-placed and most productive espionage agents of the Civil War."[8]

Because so little is known about her life, it was easy for false information to circulate. For example, recent reserach has shown that her name may actually have been Mary Jane Richards Denman. As new facts are uncovered, a clearer picture of her life and service is sure to emerge.

"The Moses of Her People"

Harriet Tubman is best known for helping hundreds of slaves escape their masters via the Underground Railroad. After escaping herself in 1849, Tubman returned to Maryland to rescue family members and soon went on to help others escape. In all, it's estimated that Tubman guided around three hundred slaves to freedom over the course of nineteen trips in a ten-year span. She became known as "Moses," after the prophet who guided the enslaved Israelites out of Egypt, and impressively she "never lost a passenger." When the Civil War began, Tubman worked for the Union army as a cook, a nurse, and later as a scout and spy, using the skills and knowledge she'd picked up over her decade helping slaves escape from the South to the North.

A Violent Childhood

Harriet Tubman was born in 1820, the last of eleven children, on a plantation in Maryland. Both of her parents, Harriet Greene and Benjamin Ross, were slaves owned by Edward Brodas. Tubman was named

Harriet Tubman, pictured here circa 1885, escaped slavery at around age seventeen and spent most of the 1850s helping others escape to the North. She also worked for the Union army during the Civil War.

Araminta Ross and nicknamed "Minty" as a child, though as a teen she would change her name to Harriet, after her mother. Slaves were expected to work hard, even as young children, and often were subject to violence and other abuse by their masters. Tubman's family was loving, but they couldn't protect her from being sent away by Brodas. When she was just five or six years old, Tubman was hired out to a white woman as a nursemaid. Tubman was severely homesick for her family, and she did her best to be as uncooperative as possible. She was punished for her behavior, but eventually she was sent back to live with her own family on the plantation.

However, it wasn't the last time that Tubman was hired out to neighbors, and on many occasions her unruly behavior led to beatings and other forms of abuse. When she was fifteen years of age, Tubman sustained a severe head injury when an overseer hit her with a heavy weight when she attempted to block him from pursuing a runaway slave. The injury was so severe that those who witnessed it were sure Tubman would die. However, under her mother's care, she slowly recovered, though never completely. A deep scar remained on her forehead, and throughout her life she suffered from pain and other difficulties related to the injury.

Escape to Freedom

Not long after Tubman was well enough to work again, Brodas, the master of the plantation, died. In his will, Brodas decreed that none of his slaves were to be sold outside of the state of Maryland. Tubman was rented out to John Stewart, a lumber merchant.

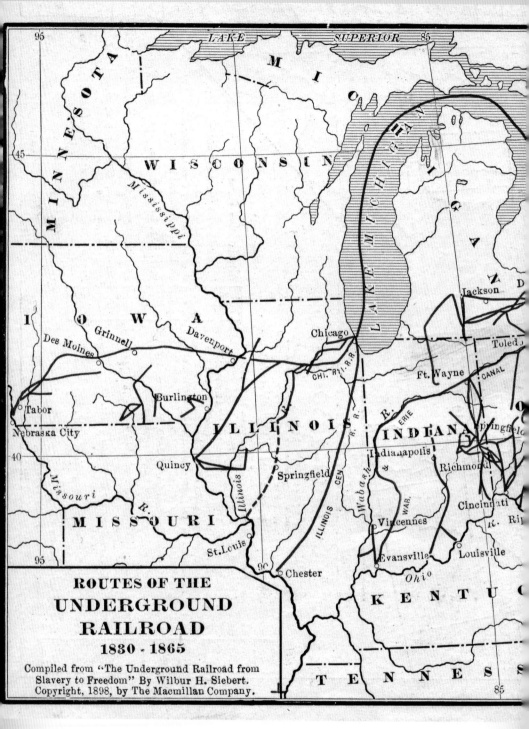

ROUTES OF THE UNDERGROUND RAILROAD 1830 - 1865

Compiled from "The Underground Railroad from Slavery to Freedom" By Wilbur H. Siebert. Copyright, 1898, by The Macmillan Company.

The Underground Railroad was a network of safe houses used by escaping slaves to travel to the Northern United States and Canada, where slavery was illegal. This map, originally published in 1920, shows many of the different routes that were available to passengers on the Underground Railroad.

The job suited her not only because she was outside, but also because Stewart allowed her to keep some of the money she made when she took on extra work.

In 1844 or 1845, Tubman married John Tubman, a free black man. His status as a freeman encouraged Tubman to hire a lawyer to look into her own legal history. The lawyer unearthed evidence that her mother had been free since the death of a former owner. The evidence proved that

The Underground Railroad

In the early nineteenth century, the network of routes and safe houses known today as the Underground Railroad began to come into use. The network ran throughout the South, with some routes leading to Florida, which was a safe haven for escaped slaves until it was annexed by the United States in 1821, and many more leading north, through the free states and up to Canada. Slave catching was a big business at the time, so operatives of the Underground Railroad had to work in secret. They also had specific names based on railway terminology—guides like Harriet Tubman were known as "conductors," while safe houses were called "stations," and the escaped slaves themselves were called "passengers." Thus Harriet Tubman's famous quote: "I was the conductor of the Underground Railroad for eight years, and I can say what most conductors can't say—I never ran my train off the track and I never lost a passenger."

Tubman should not have been born a slave. She began to contemplate her freedom.

When the heir to the Brodas estate died, rumors began to fly that the new owner would disregard Brodas's decree. Certain that her sale was imminent, Tubman suggested to her husband that they plan an escape to the North. Not only was he against the idea, but he told her that he would tell her master as soon as he discovered that she had escaped.

Tubman felt badly betrayed, but her husband's threat did not change her mind, except that from then on she plotted her escape in secret. In her first attempt to flee, she brought her three brothers with her, but not long into their journey, they grew scared and forced Tubman to return to the plantation. She was furious but kept her anger at bay and continued to plot her escape.

When the chance arose, Tubman took flight on her own. She made her escape via the Underground Railroad and, after several days of travel, arrived in Philadelphia as a free woman. But Tubman's status wouldn't last long. In an effort to appease Southern plantation owners, who were angered by the number of escaped slaves, the government passed the Fugitive Slave Act, which declared that by law escaped slaves were still considered to be slaves and could be captured and returned to their owners.

The new law did not frighten Tubman, much less cause her to emigrate to Canada, where escaped slaves could still live freely. Instead, she was inspired to return to Maryland to help guide other slaves to freedom. As the Civil War drew closer, despite the price on her head, she worked as a public speaker at abolitionist and women's rights meetings.

A Scout and a Spy

In November 1860, shortly after Abraham Lincoln was elected president, South Carolina seceded from the Union. Knowing that war was imminent, Tubman, who was living in Boston at the time, let it be known that she was very much interested in helping the Union's cause.

In 1862, Governor John Albion Andrew of Massachusetts requested that Tubman act as a nurse and teacher to a large group of slaves in Beaufort, South Carolina, who had been left behind when their owners fled the advance of Union troops. This appointment marked Tubman's first official act in her career as a Union nurse, spy, and scout.

The following year, she was able to make use of her skills navigating unknown territories, both acting as a scout and organizing a group of black scouts and spies. Led by Colonel James Montgomery, Tubman's first mission was as a scout on the Combahee River expedition. Their mission was to destroy the Confederate army's bridges and railroads, with the goal of slowing down the enemy's ability to receive supplies.

Upon seeing the Union's boats advancing down the river, slaves who were working nearby rushed down to the riverside. About eight hundred slaves crowded the banks with their hands raised. They were all taken aboard boats and transported south to Beaufort.

Subsequently, Tubman was often sent into the rebel lines as a spy. Author Sarah Bradford interviewed Tubman at length for the book *Harriet Tubman: The Moses of Her People*. Bradford wrote: "[Tubman] has been in battle when the shot was falling like hail, and the bodies of dead and wounded men were dropping around her like

The top image from this page in *Harper's Weekly*, dated July 4, 1864, is an engraving of the Union army's raid on a rice plantation along the Combahee River.

RAID OF SECOND SOUTH CAROLINA VOLUNTEERS (COL. MONTGOMERY) AMONG THE RICE PLANTATIONS ON THE COMBAHEE, S. C.—[SEE PAGE 427.]

A TYPICAL NEGRO.

We publish herewith three portraits, from photographs by M'Pherson and Oliver, of the negro GORDON, who escaped from his master in Mississippi, and came into our lines at Baton Rouge in March last. One of these portraits represents the man as he entered our lines, with clothes torn and covered with mud and dirt from his long race through the swamps and bayous, chased as he had been for days and nights by his master with several neighbors and a pack of blood-hounds; another shows him as he underwent the surgical examination previous to being mustered into the service —his back furrowed and scarred with the traces of a whipping administered on Christmas-day last; and the third represents him in United States uniform, bearing the musket and prepared for duty.

This negro displayed unusual intelligence. In order to foil the scent of the blood-hounds who were chasing him he took from his plantation onions, which he carried in his pockets. After crossing each creek or swamp he rubbed his body freely with these onions, and thus, no doubt frequently threw the dogs off the scent.

At one time in Louisiana he served our troops

as guide, and on one expedition was unfortunately taken prisoner by the rebels, who, infuriated beyond measure, tied him up and beat him, leaving him for dead. He came to life, however, and once more made his escape to our lines.

By way of illustrating the degree of brutality which slavery has developed among the whites in the section of country from which this negro came, we append the following extract from a letter in the New York *Times*, recounting what was told by

the refugees from Mrs. GILLESPIE's estate on the Black River:

The treatment of the slaves, they say, has been growing worse and worse for the last six or seven years.

Flogging with a leather strap on the naked body is common; also, paddling the body with a hand-saw until the skin is a mass of blisters, and then breaking the blisters with the teeth of the saw. They have very often seen slaves stretched out upon the ground with hands and feet held down by fellow-slaves, or lashed to stakes driven into the ground for "burning." Handfuls of dry corn-husks are then lighted, and the burning embers are whipped off with a stick so as to fall in showers of live sparks upon the naked back. This is continued until the victim is covered with blisters. If in his writhings of torture the slave gets his hand free to brush off the fire, the burning brand is applied to them.

Another method of punishment, which is inflicted for the higher order of crimes, such as running away, or other refractory conduct, is to dig a hole in the ground large enough for the slave to squat or sit down in. The victim is then stripped naked and placed in the hole, and a covering or grating of green sticks is laid over the opening. Upon this a quick fire is built, and the fire embers sifted through upon the naked flesh of the slave, until his body is blistered and swollen almost to bursting. With just enough of life to enable him to crawl, the slave is then allowed to recover from his wounds if he can, or to end his sufferings by death.

"Charley Bis" and "Overton," two hands, were both murdered by these cruel tortures. "Bis" was whipped to death, dying under the infliction, or soon after punishment. "Overton" was laid naked upon his face and burned as above described, so that the cords of his legs and the

GORDON AS HE ENTERED OUR LINES.

GORDON UNDER MEDICAL INSPECTION.

GORDON IN HIS UNIFORM AS A U. S. SOLDIER.

leaves in autumn; but the thought of fear never seems to have had place for a moment in her mind. She had her duty to perform, and she expected to be taken care of till it was done."[1]

Activism and the End of the War

When the war ended, Tubman returned to Auburn, New York, where her parents lived in a home she had purchased for them not long after she had secured their freedom in 1857. She brought with her a bundle of letters and recommendations from officers for whom she had served. In one letter written by Colonel Montgomery, dated July, 6, 1863, he referred to her as "a most remarkable woman, and invaluable as a scout."[2]

In 1869, Tubman married again. Her husband, Nelson Davis, was more than twenty years younger than Tubman. He struggled with tuberculosis, which he contracted while serving in the Civil War. They adopted a child, Gertie, in 1874. With her husband unable to work, Tubman repeatedly applied for a pension and back pay to reimburse her for those years she had served with the Union forces. The government finally granted her request in 1899, eleven years after Davis had passed away.

In the final years of her life, Tubman remained committed to the lives of people who struggled. She strongly supported women's suffrage and traveled up and down the East Coast to speak about the importance of securing voting rights. In 1903, she turned her home over to a church in order for it to be used as a home for the poor and homeless. She lived there until she died at the age of ninety-two on March 10, 1913.

Recognition of her service during the war came with her death, and she was given a funeral with semi-military honors. In 2016, the administration of President Barack Obama announced a plan to redesign the twenty-dollar bill, replacing the image of Andrew Jackson with one of Tubman. This would make Tubman the first African American to appear on US paper currency. In 2019, however, Steven Mnuchin, the treasury secretary under President Donald Trump, announced that the release of the redesigned bill would be postponed from 2020 to 2028.

The Spy of the Cumberland

Remembered by many as one of the most successful spies of the Civil War, Pauline Cushman was an actress who worked as a Union spy. In fact, her espionage career is said to have begun during a performance, when she was dared by Confederate officers to toast their president, Jefferson Davis. Cushman did so and used this toast and other similar stunts to ingratiate herself with Confederate sympathizers and officials. Since she spent much of her youth in the South, Cushman was able to travel throughout the Confederacy without arousing suspicion, easily gathering information and passing it on to the Union army. She was so successful that she was awarded an honorary rank of major in the federal army. Unfortunately, her life after the war became very difficult, and she died of a morphine overdose in 1893.

From New Orleans to New York

The daughter of a Spanish tradesman, Cushman was born Harriet Wood on June 10, 1833, in New Orleans, where even as a child she had an adventurous spirit, preferring to play the rough-and-tumble games of boys. As a young girl, she had a reputation for being a skilled shooter and an expert horsewoman. When Cushman was in her teens, her family moved to Grand Rapids, Michigan.

Pauline Cushman poses here in an army uniform, including a sword. Born Harriet Wood in New Orleans, she took her stage name when she began acting in New York in the 1860s.

Once there, she found that she had outgrown the activities that so entertained her as a youngster. She became restless and bored of Grand Rapids, then just a small frontier town located in a largely rural region. By the time Cushman was eighteen, she had had enough. She ran away to New York City to pursue a career in acting.

Soon after arriving in New York, she took on the stage name of Pauline Cushman and found a small degree of success as a stage actress. While in New York, she also fell in love with a musician and teacher named Charles Dickinson, who was also a member of the regimental band of the Forty-First Ohio Infantry.

The two married in 1853. Their wedding was held in a hotel in New Orleans, where they settled and had two children. When both of their children died in infancy, the couple moved to Cleveland, Ohio, where Dickinson enlisted as a soldier for the Union, but he was discharged from the army within months because of illness. Within two years of the start of the war, Dickinson had died.

The Stage Actress Becomes a Spy

Without a husband or children, Cushman threw herself into her acting career and joined a touring theatrical company. While performing in Louisville, Kentucky, she was offered a challenge that she would use to catapult herself into the thick of the Civil War as a spy: charmed by her good looks and talent, several Confederates offered her $300 to toast Jefferson Davis and the Confederacy just before a performance one evening.

It's possible her challengers knew her sympathies with the Union and were testing her loyalty to the South (Kentucky did not join the Confederacy, though many of its residents were Confederate sympathizers), but perhaps they simply wanted to see the actress honor their president. Whatever their intentions, the quick-thinking Cushman saw an opportunity to take up the battle for the Union. Cushman immediately notified the local Union marshal to let them know of the request. Given her background, it was clear that she had the potential to do espionage work, but before she received the go-ahead, it was decided that she would have to take an oath of loyalty to the Union.

Cushman eagerly complied with the requirement, and the following night, she took the stage and proposed a toast to Jefferson Davis and the Confederacy. Fighting in the theater broke out following her announcement, and Cushman was subsequently fired by the theater. She couldn't have been more delighted with this outcome, and thus began her career as a Civil War spy.

The Little Major

Cushman's career in espionage was short, but productive. She informed on other spies and sympathizers, assisted army police, and reported useful information about troop movements, strategies, and supplies. But as the number of missions Cushman completed grew, so did suspicion of her true intentions.

She was transferred to Nashville, Tennessee. There she worked for a general named William Rosecrans and spent several months with the Army of the Cumberland. While General Rosecrans was preparing a campaign to drive Confederate general Braxton Briggs across the Tennessee River in 1863, Cushman was sent into Confederate lines to determine the whereabouts and abilities of the Tennessee army.

William Rosecrans was, at various points in his life, an inventor, company executive, and politician, but he first became famous as a general in the Union army.

General Rosecrans

William Rosecrans held numerous roles over his lifetime, including diplomat, politician, company executive, inventor, and officer. Born in 1819, he attended the United States Military Academy and did very well there, despite having little formal education. In fact, he became a professor at the academy after graduating. When the Civil War broke out, Rosecrans was assigned to work with General George McClellan in Ohio, and when McClellan was sent to Washington, Rosecrans took over his post as commander of the area that would become known as West Virginia. After the war, Rosecrans became an ambassador to Mexico, and later on, a congressman for California. Rosecrans passed away in 1898, seemingly from grief over his grandchild, who died of diphtheria.

In 1865, the final year of the Civil War, time was running out for Cushman. Although she gathered important information for several weeks, Confederate soldiers finally captured her. Using her skills as an actress, she feigned illness and, when the opportunity arose, managed to break away from her captors.

The escape was short-lived, and within days, the same soldiers captured her again. A search of Cushman's belongings revealed that she was in possession of drawings she had stolen from an army engineer. She was promptly arrested. Weakened by fever, Cushman was too ill to attend her own trial. Her jailer kept her abreast of court proceedings. The court found her guilty and sentenced her to death by hanging, with instructions that the sentence be carried out immediately.

Never one to give up easily, Cushman calmly plotted out her last deceit. In an odd show of sympathy, perhaps because she was a woman, the court granted Cushman a stay of execution until she was fully recovered from her illness. Once again, falling back on her flair for the dramatic, Cushman was able to convince her captors that she was ill well after she was on the road to recovery.

Her ploy was starting to wear thin when the Union army invaded Cumberland, Tennessee, the city in which she was being held. General William Rosecrans's advance guard spared her life as the Confederates retreated. She was freed. After her rescue, Secretary of War Edwin Stanton appointed her a major in the US Army, and President Lincoln referred to her as "the little major."[1] Cushman was soon appreciated throughout the North.

Fame and Struggles After the War

In the years following the war, her heroic efforts were described in several articles and books, including *The Life of Pauline Cushman*, written from Cushman's notes by Ferdinand Sarmiento in 1865. Many of the book's more colorful details have been discounted in recent years. For example, though the story of Cushman starting her career by offering an onstage toast may be a dramatic one, it is believed by some that she was "already a secret agent when she toasted Jefferson Davis and the Confederacy from a Louisville stage."[2]

After the war, Cushman returned to the stage with limited success. She also capitalized on her experience as a spy. Under the name of Spy of the Cumberland, she began lecturing. By 1872, her speaking engagements brought her to California. Cushman was well known for her

Edwin Stanton was an attorney and politician. He served as the attorney general from 1860 to 1861 and as secretary of war under both Abraham Lincoln and his successor, Andrew Johnson.

fiery temper, which came to light when several California newspapers questioned her identity as a former spy. Upon learning of their doubts, she reportedly "threatened to horsewhip one of the paper's editors."[3]

Struggling financially, Cushman applied for a pension based on her service as a secret agent during the war. Despite being commissioned a major, she received only a monthly pension because of the time that her husband had served.

She married August Fitcher the same year she arrived in San Francisco. Her government pension ceased when she remarried, and within seven years her second husband died. Not long after his death, she took a third husband, though this union did not last either. After several unhappy years, she left him.

Cushman's life became less and less happy over the years. Eking out an existence as a maid, she became addicted to morphine. Several accounts describe her death on December 2, 1893, as a suicide. However, the local coroner ruled that the cause of death was "from morphine taken, not with suicidal intent, but to relieve pain."[4]

The Grand Army of the Republic gave Cushman a full military funeral, which was attended by more than eight hundred veterans. She was buried in a military cemetery with a headstone that read, "Pauline Cushman, Federal Spy and Scout of the Cumberland."[5]

Alias Frank Thompson

It is estimated that over four hundred women disguised themselves as men and enlisted as soldiers on both sides during the Civil War. One of the most famous of these women was Sarah Emma Edmonds, a Canadian-born woman who dressed as a man and enlisted as a male nurse in the Union army. By the time she enlisted, Edmonds already had a history of dressing as a man: after escaping an arranged marriage, she disguised herself as a man and became a Bible salesman using the name Frank Thompson. This disguise allowed her to travel and find work far more easily than she might have as a woman, given the expectations and rights of women at the time.

After leaving the army, Edmonds wrote a memoir about her military experiences, which was published in 1865 and entitled *Nurse and Spy in the Union Army*. In the book, Edmonds claimed that she had also worked undercover as a spy, using all manner of disguises to collect information on behalf of the Union. Today, her memoir is largely considered fictional, although it's believed that Edmonds did carry out a few intelligence missions while posing as Frank Thompson. Despite the fact that the stories she told are likely invented, her narrative does tell us a lot about what it might have been like to spy for the Union army during the Civil War.

A Tomboy in New Brunswick

Sarah Emma Edmonds's father, Isaac Edmonson, immigrated to New Brunswick from Scotland in the early 1800s and eventually married Elizabeth Leeper, who came to Canada via Ireland. Elizabeth bore six children, five girls and one boy. Sarah, who would be known by her middle name, Emma, was born in December 1841 and was the youngest girl. She and her siblings attended school at a one-room schoolhouse, and each Sunday the family attended an Anglican church.

Edmonds was a spirited little girl. In addition to the hard work she did helping her father run his farm, she enjoyed swimming, riding horses, and hunting. Though it was common for farm girls to partake in all of these activities, Edmonds was much more active and mischievous than her siblings, including her younger brother. Recalling her childhood in a diary, she wrote, "I heard my mother once tell a Scotch Presbyterian clergyman that she was afraid I would meet with some violent death, for I was always in some unheard of mischief."[1]

Edmonds's friendly demeanor would lead her to make influential relationships throughout her life, but it was a chance meeting with a peddler who visited their farm that would change her view on her own destiny. Charmed by Edmonds, who generously invited him to stay for dinner, the peddler returned her kindness with the gift of a book, *Fanny Campbell, the Female Pirate Captain*. Edmonds immediately became entranced by the book's brave and daring hero. Sylvia Dannet writes:

> At the point in the book where the heroine, Fanny Campbell, in a plot to save her imprisoned lover,

Portrait of the Female Pirate.

BY LIEUTENANT MURRAY.

BOSTON:
PUBLISHED BY F. GLEASON, 1 1-2 TREMONT ROW.
1845.

Jones, Printer, 42 Congress Street.

Fanny Campbell, the Female Pirate Captain was a popular 1844 novel about a woman who goes to sea to rescue her childhood sweetheart.

cut off her auburn curls, put on her blue jacket and "stepped into the freedom and glorious independence of masculinity," Emma flung her straw hat into the air and shouted in excitement. "Someday I will follow Fanny Campbell's example!"[2]

When Edmonds turned fifteen, she found herself being pursued by an older farmer who lived nearby. Edmonds was appalled by his advances as well as her father's approval of his actions and insistence that preparations be made for the two to wed. Some sources say that Edmonds's father was actually indebted to the man, and that the marriage was arranged to help make up for the money he owed. Regardless, Edmonds's mother disapproved of the marriage and made plans for her daughter to leave the farm with a trusted friend just one day before the wedding. When Edmonds left her family behind, she also left her past behind, including changing her name from Edmonson to Edmonds.

Frank Thompson, the Bible Salesman

After leaving her family, Edmonds lived with her mother's friend Annie Moffitt in Salisbury, a lively town in Canada located near the US border. She worked in Moffitt's millinery shop and quickly became a favorite among its visitors. Several years after her arrival, however, Edmonds learned that her father knew of her whereabouts and was planning to come and bring her back to the family farm. Terrified that he might still insist upon the marriage from which she had fled, she began to plan an escape that would free her from his influence forever. Following the lead of her favorite storybook heroine, Edmonds made her escape dressed as a man. She wasn't content, however, to use her disguise just to run away. She took Fanny's lead one step further by assuming the full identity of a man. Known as Frank Thompson to her new friends and acquaintances, she took on a job as a Bible salesman. Her new identity must have been a good one, for within the company her reputation was only that of an excellent employee.

Maintaining her identity as a man, Edmonds eventually traveled to the United States, where she felt the opportunities to make money as a salesman were much better than in Canada. She ended up in Michigan, where she continued to sell Bibles.

When the Civil War began, Edmonds could have returned to Canada, but instead she chose to enlist in the army. Since she was vehemently opposed to slavery, there was never any question that she would enlist with the Union army.

Enlistment and Espionage

When President Abraham Lincoln put out a call for volunteers, "Frank" went to the recruitment center in Flint, Michigan. While no one doubted that she was a man, she was turned away because she did not meet the military's height requirement. She persisted and, several months after her first attempt, was drafted as a male nurse with the rank of private.

In July 1860, Edmonds received her first active duty assignment when her unit was called upon to fight in the First Battle of Bull Run. The outcome was a bloody one, with many soldiers injured and killed. In the days that

Edmonds immigrated to the United States from Canada. She disguised herself as a man named Frank Thompson, as seen here, to make traveling easier.

followed, Edmonds attended the wounded in a hospital located in the nation's capital.

When a soldier with whom she had become close was shot and killed, Edmonds was inspired to avenge his death by taking on a more active role in the military. When she heard that there was a vacancy for a spy in the Union's Secret Service division, she immediately applied for the position. Her exploits as a spy are disputed. Much of our knowledge of her covert activities comes from her 1865 memoir *Nurse and Spy,* which has come to be recognized as primarily fiction.

The First Mission

Though *Nurse and Spy* is mostly fictional, it's very possible that Edmonds wrote of events that she'd witnessed.

Examining the Historical Record

Though her personal accounts of being a spy are disputed, it seems that Edmonds did conduct at least two intelligence missions for the Union army while enlisted as Frank Thompson. For these, she "disguised" herself as a woman. It may be that other parts of her narrative in *Nurse and Spy* are true, but historians are still separating fact from fiction. In fact, it can be difficult to know what really happened at any point in history beyond living memory, since even the most "objective" records can still reflect the biases and beliefs of their creators. Separating out the facts in the history of secret intelligence can be particularly difficult, since secrets and lies are so important in espionage, and many spies erased or falsified records in order to escape being identified.

This engraving shows Edmonds on horseback carrying the American flag with troops and tents in the background, during the time she was working as a nurse in the Union army.

Though she didn't actually collect information disguised as a black man or an Irishwoman as she claimed, the tales she tells can teach us about what it was like to spy for the Union, even if the details aren't necessarily accurate.

On what Edmonds describes as her "first mission," she was instructed to enter Confederate territory and gather information about the enemy's plans. She claimed that in order to carry out the mission, she had to disguise herself as a black man, using iodine to dye her skin. "With a few hard crackers in my pocket and my revolver loaded and capped, I started on foot without even a blanket or anything which might create suspicion."[3] After a day of traveling south toward Richmond, Virginia, she allegedly encountered a half-dozen slaves who were responsible for bringing food and supplies to a group of Confederate soldiers who were assigned to watch for advancing federal troops. Soldiers with guard postings like this were called pickets.

As the story goes, when an officer approached her and asked her to identify herself, she replied that she was a freeman on her way to Richmond in search of work. Told by the officer that there were no free black men in Virginia, she was immediately put to work building a stone wall to protect Confederate soldiers from enemy fire. At night, while everyone else slept, Edmonds took notes on the Confederate army's supplies and weapons.

After another day of hard work delivering water to soldiers, in the evening she was put to work carrying supplies to the pickets. In an effort to garner more information, Edmonds conversed for as long as possible with each soldier she visited. An officer noticed her dawdling and ordered her to take the post of a Confederate soldier who had recently been shot.

In the story, Edmonds took the post happily, knowing that it would provide the perfect opportunity to escape to the nearby federal camp. It was a cloudy, damp night. It began to rain, and the pickets on either side of her had taken shelter under trees. Noiselessly, grasping a Confederate rifle as a trophy, Edmonds walked through the woods toward the Union lines. She knew the federal pickets would fire on anybody moving toward them, so she bedded down for the remainder of the night within hailing distance of the Union picket line. Edmonds wrote that her first successfully completed mission, though dangerous, whetted her appetite to do more reconnaissance work.

The Second Mission

In the tale of her second assignment, Edmonds describes dressing as an old Irishwoman who made her living by traveling from city to city selling baked goods. Not long after crossing into Confederate territory, the story goes, she came upon an abandoned house in which she found a Confederate soldier on the verge of death. She comforted him as best she could in his final hours, and not long before he died, he requested that she deliver his watch and some papers to his commanding officer.

She set out for the deceased soldier's camp in the morning and soon saw a sentinel on the road ahead. Edmonds stopped to gather her thoughts, and while she rested she concluded that her story would be that much more believable if it appeared she had been grieving over the soldier's death. Ever the actress, she rubbed a pinch of pepper in her eyes, and within minutes, it appeared as though she had been crying for hours.

81

Artillerymen of the Union army pose with a 24-pounder gun in September 1861 in Virginia.

In her diary, she describes the event: "I took from my basket the black pepper and sprinkled a little of it on my pocket handkerchief, which I applied to my eyes."[4] As she tells it, the tears worked perfectly, and the soldier allowed her to pass without hesitation. In fact, so convinced was he of her sad tale that before she left he shared with her his unit's plans to fight off the enemy.

While waiting for the return of the dead soldier's commanding officer, she managed to gather more details on the Confederacy's plans. When the opportunity arose, she made her getaway laden with important information that would ultimately save the lives of many soldiers.

Leaving the Army

While in the military, Edmonds continued in her role as nurse as needed during battles. She had a reputation for seeking out medical supplies and food for injured and underfed troops. When she wasn't needed as a nurse, she carried mail between camps. Near the start of the Second Battle of Bull Run, fought on August 29 and 30, 1862, her leg was badly injured when she was thrown from her horse while delivering the mail. Despite the fact that she could barely walk, she kept up her responsibilities as a mail carrier, only asking for assistance in mounting or dismounting her horse.

Edmonds's last supposed mission took place in Louisville, Kentucky. Though under Union command, the people who lived there supported the Confederacy, and Edmonds was sent there to dig up any information she could on counterspy activity. Not long after her arrival, she was hired as a clerk in a dry goods store, "where she proved to be such an efficient worker that her employer asked her if she would like to go out to the nearest Confederate camps and sell merchandise to the soldiers."[5] According to her account, in no time she was able to uncover the names and whereabouts of three Confederate spies, two of whom were ultimately arrested.

In April 1863, Edmonds became severely ill. This time, she was unable to shake off her illness and carry on as she had done on so many past occasions. She requested a two-week leave, which was denied, leaving her with the sole option of convalescing in a hospital. Concerned that her true identity might be discovered, she made the decision to go AWOL and abandon her military career forever.

Nurse and Spy and Later Life

She wasn't quite ready to give up her disguise as Frank Thompson, though, and it was several more months before she would reclaim her female identity as Sarah Emma Edmonds. When she recovered her health and identity, she began work on her exaggerated memoir, *Nurse and Spy in the Union Army*, which was published in 1865 and became an immediate best seller.

Shortly after her book was published, Edmonds met and married Linus Seely (which she later changed to Seelye), also a Canadian. She gave birth to three children and adopted two boys, though three of her children died young.

As the years passed by, she grew increasingly uncomfortable with the manner in which she had left behind her military career. Not only did she not receive any sort of wages or pension, but Frank Thompson was still officially listed as a deserter.

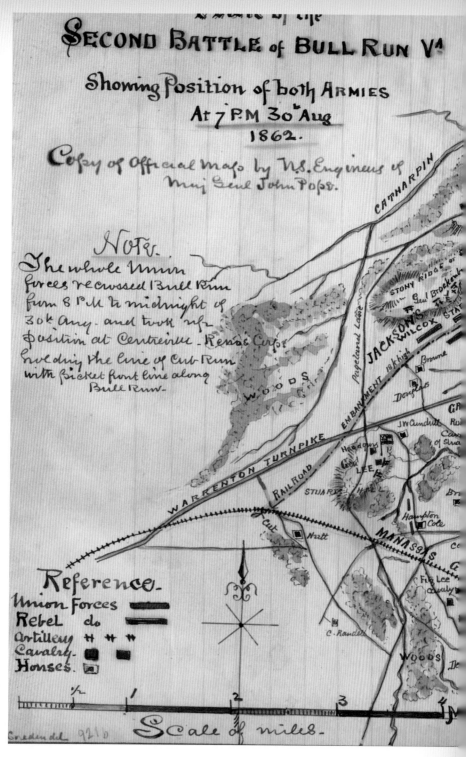

This sketch of the Second Battle of Bull Run displays the positioning and movements of both armies around 7 p.m. on August 30, 1862, with the Union forces marked in purple and Confederates in red.

Twenty years after she left the army, Edmonds began a campaign to both receive any payment to which she was entitled as well as to have the status of deserter removed from "Frank's" records.

It took many years of hard work and persistence, but eventually Edmonds was recognized for her service as a nurse in Company F, Second Regiment, Michigan Volunteer Infantry. "On April 2, 1889—seven years after she had first begun to seek government aid and the clearance of her name in the army records—[Edmonds] was restored to honorable standing on the records of the War Department, granted an honorable discharge and her back pay and bounty."[6]

Edmonds died at the age of fifty-seven due to complications from the illness that originally drove her to leave the military. Though she was first buried in La Porte, Texas, her remains were later moved to Washington Cemetery, a military burial place in Houston.

Chronology

1807 Congress bans the importation of slaves into the country, effective on January 1, 1808.

1850 The Fugitive Slave Act is passed. It allows for the arrest or capture of fugitive slaves in all states, colonies, and territories.

1852 Harriet Beecher Stowe publishes *Uncle Tom's Cabin* in response to the pro-slavery movement.

1857 In the Dred Scott decision, the Supreme Court rules that black people are not U.S. citizens, and thus slaveholders could travel openly with them to free states and territories without the fear of being sued.

1860 **November** Abraham Lincoln is elected the sixteenth president of the United States. In several states in the Deep South, his name is not included on the ballot.

December South Carolina becomes the first state to secede from the Union.

1861 **January–February** Six more states— Mississippi, Alabama, Florida, Georgia, Louisiana, and Texas—secede from the Union. With South Carolina, they form a provisional government, the Confederate States of America.

February Jefferson Davis is unanimously elected president of the Confederacy by state delegates.

April 12 Confederate soldiers fire on Fort Sumter, South Carolina, and the war officially begins.

April 17 Virginia secedes.

May Three more states—Arkansas, North Carolina, and Tennessee—secede and join the Confederacy.

June 10 Federal prisoners start to arrive in Richmond, Virginia, following the Battle of Big Bethel.

July Union forces under General Irvin McDowell are defeated at the First Battle of Bull Run.

November Lincoln appoints General George B. McClellan commander in chief of the Union armies.

1862 June–July McClellan loses the Seven Days Battle east of Richmond.

July Lincoln promotes General Henry Halleck to command all Union armies, demoting McClellan to command the Army of the Potomac.

August The Second Battle of Bull Run occurs.

September General McClellan wards off the Confederates, under General Robert E. Lee in the Battle of Antietam—the bloodiest day of fighting in American history.

1863 Mary Elizabeth Bowser starts working in the Davis household.

January 1 Lincoln formally signs the Emancipation Proclamation into law.

November 21 Lincoln delivers the Gettysburg Address.

1864 January Sylvanius Thompson, Sarah's husband, is executed by General John Hunt Morgan and his men.

March Lincoln appoints Ulysses S. Grant commander of all US armies.

September 4 General Morgan is killed, in part due to Sarah Thompson's information.

November Lincoln is elected president for a second term.

1865 *Nurse and Spy in the Union Army* by Sarah Emma Edmonds is published.

January The House of Representatives votes to pass the Thirteenth Amendment, which abolishes slavery.

April 9 General Lee surrenders to General Grant at Appomattox Court House in Virginia.

April 14 President Lincoln is assassinated.

April–May Remaining Confederate forces surrender.

December 18 The Thirteenth Amendment is ratified, officially outlawing slavery.

Chapter Notes

Chapter 1

The Union's Angel of Revenge

1. Sarah Thompson, transcribed by Joan Yehl, "Sarah Thompson's account of Morgan's Defeat, September 3, 1864," *Sarah E. Thompson Papers, 1859-1898*, Duke University, https://library.duke.edu/rubenstein/ scriptorium/thompson/1864-09-03/1864-09-03 -transcript.html (retrieved April 21, 2019).
2. Sarah Thompson, "Letter to Hon. John Sherman from Sarah Thompson, April 19, 1879," *Sarah E. Thompson Papers, 1859-1898*, Duke University, https://library.duke.edu/rubenstein/scriptorium/ thompson/1879-04-19/1879-04-19.html (retrieved April 21, 2019).
3. Thompson trans. Yehl.
4. Larry G. Eggleston, *Women in the Civil War: Extraordinary Stories of Soldiers, Spies, Nurses, Doctors, Crusaders, and Others* (Jefferson, NC: McFarland & Company, 2003), p. 162.
5. Thompson, "Letter to Hon. John Sherman from Sarah Thompson: April 19, 1879."

Chapter 2

The Abolitionist Southern Belle

1. Larry G. Eggleston, *Women in the Civil War: Extraordinary Stories of Soldiers, Spies, Nurses, Doctors, Crusaders, and Others* (Jefferson, NC: McFarland & Company, 2003), p. 80.

2. Alan Axelrod, *The War Between the Spies: A History of Espionage During the American Civil War* (Boston: Atlantic Monthly Press, 1992), p. 104.

3. Elizabeth L. Van Lew, *A Yankee Spy in Richmond: The Civil War Diary of "Crazy Bet" Van Lew*, edited by David D. Ryan (Mechanicsburg, PA: Stackpole Books, 1996), p. 27.

4. Harnett T. Kane, "Spies for the Blue and Gray," http://www.civilwarhome.com/crazybet.htm (retrieved April 21, 2019).

5. Van Lew, p. 8.

6. Van Lew, p. 11.

7. Eggleston, p. 82.

8. Eggleston, p. 82.

9. Eggleston, p. 83.

10. Eggleston, p. 84.

Chapter 3

In the House of the Enemy

1. Elaine Schneider, "Civil War Heroines: Information on Sojourner Truth, Rebecca Wright and Mary Todd Lincoln," http://www.essortment.com/civil-war-women -information-sojourner-truth-rebecca-wright-mary-todd -lincoln-21018.html (retrieved April 21, 2019).

2. Elizabeth L. Van Lew, *A Yankee Spy in Richmond: The Civil War Diary of "Crazy Bet" Van Lew*, edited by David D. Ryan (Mechanicsburg, PA: Stackpole Books, 1996), p. 11.

3. Van Lew, p. 11.

4. Van Lew, p. 12.

5. Bonnie V. Winston, "Mary Elizabeth Bowser," *Richmond Times Dispatch*, February 10, 1998, https://www.richmond.com/special-section/black -history/mary-elizabeth-bowser/article_54f489b4

-6090-53c7-8c52-db1c8f07a5c1.html (retrieved April 21, 2019).

6. Vertamae Grosvenor, "The Spy Who Served Me," NPR, April 19, 2002, https://www.npr.org/templates/story/story.php?storyId=1141977 (retrieved April 21, 2019).

7. Grosvenor, "The Spy Who Served Me."

8. Winston, "Mary Elizabeth Bowser."

Chapter 4

"The Moses of Her People"

1. Sarah Bradford, *Harriet Tubman: The Moses of Her People* (Bedford, MA: Applewood Books, 1886), p. 100.

2. Jone Johnson Lewis, "Harriet Tubman—Moses of Her People," ThoughtCo, https://www.thoughtco.com/harriet-tubman-biography-3529273 (retrieved April 21, 2019).

Chapter 5

The Spy of the Cumberland

1. Carolyn Swift, "Cushman, Civil War Spy, Is a SLV Legend," *Santa Cruz Sentinel* (Santa Cruz, CA), March 12, 2000.

2. Larry G. Eggleston, *Women in the Civil War: Extraordinary Stories of Soldiers, Spies, Nurses, Doctors, Crusaders, and Others* (Jefferson, NC: McFarland & Company, 2003), p. 126.

3. Swift, "Cushman, Civil War Spy, Is a SLV Legend."

4. Eggleston, p. 127.

5. Mary Elizabeth Massey, *Women in the Civil War* (Lincoln, NE: University of Nebraska Press, 1966), p. 102.

Chapter 6
Alias Frank Thompson

1. Sarah Emma Edmonds, *Nurse and Spy in the Union Army* (Scituate, MA: Digital Scanning, 2000), p. 218.
2. Sylvia G. Dannet, *She Rode with the Generals: The True and Incredible Story of Sarah Emma Seelye, Alias Franklin Thompson* (New York: Thomas Nelson and Sons, 1960), pp. 24–25.
3. Dannet, p. 27.
4. Edmonds, p. 163.
5. Dannet, p. 224.
6. Dannet, p. 275.

Glossary

abolitionism A movement to abolish, or end, slavery. A person opposed to slavery was known as an abolitionist.

bondage Enslavement.

cipher A method of transforming text in order to conceal its meaning.

Civil War The conflict from 1861 to 1865 between the North (the Union) and the South (the Confederacy), which had seceded from the Union. Also known as the War of the Rebellion and the War Between the States.

Confederacy The eleven Southern states that seceded from the United States in 1860 and 1861; also called the South. Members of the Confederacy were called Confederates.

demeanor A person's manner toward others.

demise The death of someone or something.

despotic Behaving like an oppressive ruler or tyrant.

destitute Altogether lacking; without a means of financial support.

espionage The act of spying.

freeman A person who is not enslaved. By the time of the Civil War, "freeman" was primarily used to refer specifically to a black person who was not a slave.

hire out To allow someone else to use a possession in exchange for some form of payment.

morphine A highly addictive opioid used for pain management.

regiment A unit of soldiers.

secede To withdraw from a group, such as a government.

suffrage The right to vote.

Underground Railroad The network of safe houses and the secret routes between them used by slaves to travel from the South to the North in the 1800s.

Union The states loyal to the federal government headed by President Abraham Lincoln during the Civil War; the North.

Bibliography

Abbott, Karen. *Liar, Temptress, Soldier, Spy: Four Women Undercover in the Civil War.* New York: Harper, 2014.

Axelrod, Alan. *The War Between the Spies: A History of Espionage During the American Civil War.* Boston: Atlantic Monthly Press, 1992.

Blanton, Deanne, and Lauren M. Cook. *They Fought Like Demons: Women Soldiers in the American Civil War.* Baton Rouge, LA: Louisiana State University Press, 2002.

Bradford, Sarah. *Harriet Tubman: The Moses of Her People.* Bedford, MA: Applewood Books, 1886.

Dannet, Sylvia G. *She Rode with the Generals: The True and Incredible Story of Sarah Emma Seelye, Alias Franklin Thompson.* New York: Thomas Nelson and Sons, 1960.

Eggleston, Larry G. *Women in the Civil War: Extraordinary Stories of Soldiers, Spies, Nurses, Doctors, Crusaders, and Others.* Jefferson, NC: McFarland & Company, 2003.

Leonard, Elizabeth D. *Yankee Women: Gender Battles in the Civil War.* New York: W. W. Norton & Company, 1994.

Massey, Mary Elizabeth. *Women in the Civil War.* Lincoln, NE: University of Nebraska Press, 1994.

McCurry, Stephanie. *Women's War: Fighting and Surviving the American Civil War.* Boston, MA: Belknap Press, 2019.

Petry, Ann. *Harriet Tubman: Conductor on the Underground Railroad.* New York: Harper Trophy, 1996.

Van Lew, Elizabeth L., and David D. Ryan, ed. *A Yankee Spy in Richmond: The Civil War Diary of "Crazy Bet" Van Lew.* Mechanicsburg, PA: Stackpole Books, 1996.

Further Reading

Books

Bradley, Michael. *Civil War Myths and Legends: The True Stories Behind History's Mysteries.* 2nd ed. Guilford, CT: Globe Pequot Press, 2019.

Cordell, M. R. *Courageous Women of the Civil War: Soldiers, Spies, Medics, and More.* Chicago, IL: Chicago Review Press, 2016.

Cummings, Judy Dodge. *The Civil War: The Struggle That Divided America.* White River Junction, VT: Nomad Press, 2017.

Monson, Marianne. *Women of the Blue and Gray: True Stories of Mothers, Medics, Soldiers, and Spies of the Civil War.* Salt Lake City, UT: Shadow Mountain Publishing, 2018.

Petry, Ann. *Harriet Tubman: Conductor on the Underground Railroad.* New York, NY: Amistad, 2018.

Websites

American Battlefield Trust
https://www.battlefields.org
The American Battlefield Trust works to preserve battlefields around the country and has information and documents from a number of different battles and conflicts, including the Civil War.

American Civil War Museum

https://acwm.org

The American Civil War Museum has one of the largest and most thorough collections of Civil War artifacts and documents in the country, much of which can be viewed through its website.

National Women's History Museum

https://www.womenshistory.org

The website of the National Women's History Museum in Alexandria, Virginia, offers digitized exhibits, articles, and other resources about women throughout American history.

Index